How To Get Heat Without Fire

Also by Marilyn Kallet

Poetry
In the Great Night
Devils Live So Near

Translations
Last Love Poems of Paul Eluard

Anthologies
Worlds In Our Words:
Contemporary American Women Writers
(co-edited with Patricia Clark)

A House of Gathering:
Poets on May Sarton's Poetry
(editor)

Criticism
Honest Simplicity in William Carlos Williams'
"Asphodel, That Greeny Flower"

How To Get Heat Without Fire

Marilyn Kallet

NEW MESSENGER BOOKS
Publishers Of
NEW MILLENNIUM WRITINGS

ACKNOWLEDGMENTS

I am grateful to the Virginia Center for the Creative Arts, where many of these poems were written. The MacDowell Colony, Ragdale Foundation, Montalvo Center for the Arts, and Byrdcliffe Arts Colony have also offered hospitality. A Tennessee Arts Commission Literary Fellowship helped start this manuscript in 1988; both the John C. Hodges Better English Fund and the Graduate School at the University of Tennessee have supported my writing. The Squaw Valley Community of Writers enabled me to finish this manuscript in the wise presence of Sharon Olds, Galway Kinnell, Yusef Komunayakaa, and Brenda Hillman.

Over the years wonderful poets, artists and friends have offered encouragement and suggestions: Alice Friman, Joy Harjo, Tess Gallagher, Clayton Eshleman, Gioia Timpanelli, Robert Bly, Pamela Walker, Libby Jones, Dorothy Folz-Gray, Linda Parsons, Bobby Caudle Rogers, Michael Keene, Deborah Harper, Kenneth Pobo, Eric Patterson, Mariflo Stephens, Daniel Roop, Keith Norris, Heather Dobbins, Mel Rosenthal, Roberta Perry, Mindy Weisel, Katherine Kadish, and Joelle Wallach. Julia Demmin, Margo O'Malley Elledge, and Carol Devenksi have been my mainstays. May Sarton helped me to get through the difficult times.

For Lou and Heather

Even in our sleep we watch over one another.

—Paul Eluard

Some of the poems included here have been published in magazines and anthologies. Grateful acknowledgment is made to the editors.

New Letters; The Ledge; Hawaii Review; Now & Then; New Millennium Writings; International Quarterly; The Yalobusha Review; Poems and Plays; ShadowPlay; Denver Quarterly; Sulfur; The Greensboro Review; Earth's Daughters; Widener Review; Whiskey Island Magazine; Carolina Quarterly; Tendril; Plainswoman; The Greenfield Review; Ironwood; Confrontation.

Home Works: A Book of Tennessee Writers; Voices from the Valley: Selections from the Knoxville Writers' Guild; Life on the Line: Selections on Words and Healing; Fine China: Twenty Years of Earth's Daughters; All Around Us: Poems from the Valley.

The quotations in "Blues" are from Pablo Neruda and from a song by Michael Mayes, respectively.

The epigraph for "Why Not Blossom Instead?" is from a translation of Baudelaire by Robert Bly.

The epigraph for "Nothing is so White" is a reworking of a line by William Carlos Williams, from *Paterson II;* the line recurs in "December Journal."

How to Get Heat Without Fire

ISBN 1-888338-05-9
Library of Congress Catalog Card Number—96-71298—Poetry

Cover art is from an original painting, *In the Beginning,* by Helen Hightower.
Cover design by Rhonda Swicegood of Hart Graphics.
Photograph of Marilyn Kallet by Paul Efird.
Book designed and edited by Don Williams.

Published by New Messenger Books, publishers of *New Millennium Writings*. For distribution information, write PO Box 2463, Knoxville, TN 37901, or phone 423-428-0389. To order this book, enclose $12 per copy.

CONTENTS

I. Forget the Silk 9

Forget the Silk 11
Blues 12
In a Word 14
Saying Goodbye 15
A Small Lie 16
Keys to the Door of Endings 17
Moaning 18
Why I Wear My Hair Long 19
Her Ex-husband 20
A New Way 21
Mango Woman 22
Bad Sex 23

II. Double Vision 25

The White Zombie 27
The Dream 28
Letter on the Goddess 29
October Afternoon 30
Heather and the Wolf 31
Landscape With Bluebirds 32
Lovers 33
Rhinoceroses 34
After Your Visit 35
Double Vision 36
Prayer For *Chutzpah* 37
December Journal 40
Redbird 42

III. Sentimental Talk 45

Unusual 47
The Genius Test 49
Before the Discovery of the Mind 51
Passover 53
Once Upon a Time 54
Nothing is so White 55
Easy Listening Music 56
Sentimental Talk 58
The Pocketbook 59
Heaven 60
Why Not Blossom Instead? 63
Out of Bondage 64
Dear Orpheus 65

IV. How To Get Heat Without Fire 67

Fireflies 69
The Ladies 70
Black Bean Soup 71
Entering the Blue Room 73
Hunger 74
Yahrzeit, for my Father 75
The Only Way 76
Bill 77
In the Face of Solitude 78
How to Get Heat Without Fire 79

About the Author 80

I. Forget the Silk

Forget the Silk

Forget the silk of poppies, their unrelenting red, I could
take you to forgetting, lick amnesia across your lashes,
make you forget half-learned love, forget your name
and the word for blood, caress you with my breasts until you
spill your hair over me and we're lost in a silkstorm.
Forget the drained desert stars, hold me fast as constellations
you painted on your ceiling as a boy, unfold me like a true map,
wander my sleepless byways. Taste the dark-skinned girl
you used to love coming toward you without sorrow,
surprise the man you mourned hiding blues inside
his hair—we'd be the bridge drumming one world into
another, riding our breaths. Over, under, all around,
crooning our own night chant, fingering cries.
Could you bear forgetting this?

Blues

Your voice resounds
in my hands
listening with my skin
my lungs
my breath
I take your music in
and now you've got me in your palm
so close
I hear the poison.
Your blood sings everything
you've swallowed
what's been done to you
& what you won't hear:
Drown
it out.
Rage, blood beating
thrusting
what I don't
have in me.
Quiero
no que lo tengo.

City lights shimmer over the desert edges
of your moonless night.
You're fixed to the blues
glued to what you still want
stuck
stabbing yourself in the heart.
Hey, it's easy for me,
I'm flying like a hawk over a doomed city
soon your sound won't reach me
its echoes will recede.
But for you
blood is no metaphor.

If I could filter the darkness out of you
I'd do it
with my fingers, with my lips.
Then we'd play this howling storm
like a quaint souvenir from hell, as if
it were only music.
On a fragile
paper sail
you'd get out
reinvent your life—
You wrote that.
You once wrote that.

In a Word

Say "destiny"—
simply hand yourself over
to the rocks
and surge and pounding, enter
the house made of storm.

Think, "We're
inevitable
now," the way meteors
can't stop
falling.

Night doesn't need
to think.
Sun grows heedlessly
in the huge heads of flowers.
The hurricane
has to be itself, spectacular
disaster.

Afterwards
the debris
the numbness
how one can see it all
and still roll toward it
that devastating wave
relentless
tides don't care what's in them
their passionate cargo discarded
for whatever comes
what's never the same

never this
man
this woman
this wave of flesh this perfect
going under.

Saying Goodbye

We embraced, there in the parking lot
of the ordinary.
How could I know your arms were arguing last things?
Your cheek in my hair.
For a moment I pressed against you. Goodbyes can be vast.
In a breath, we traded lives. I didn't know you
were a cliff I had reached the edge of.
Your touch echoed.
I simply followed it like song.

A Small Lie

A small lie,
        an inconsistency,
you mailed the letter Tuesday
        and a tape for me,
then again maybe
        you mailed them Saturday.
Each day my mailbox holds sharp air.
        The shape of emptiness gathers,
a stiletto
        glistening in my gut.

"I fear carelessness most," you wrote.
        So do I. Though
yours is so perfectly formed
        it's hard not to see
purposefulness, art.

We have to get messy first before
        we get neat,
very very messy.
        You deepen the cut.
Blame the city you lived in,
        your friends who betrayed you,
they put the poison in your cup.
        And I helped you to arrive,
didn't I?
        Thinking it was the land of poetry,
that others before you had leaned into
        the desert's fire and soared.
Why not blame me?
        Now you'll show me how to be sick,
to want so badly you want to die.

And though I know the white lady belongs
        to you, your dream,
your favorite murdering ghost,
at night when I'm restless and so lonely
        I'm gnawing the dark
for a moment I think I'd grasp
        her sure arm.
Daylight, when I look for a letter
        with that same stupid flash of hope,
the blade's in your hand again and she's there
        breathing hard:
"He's all *mine*, sweetheart!"

Keys to the Door of Endings

I longed to talk with you about our ending,
to craft it, make it right.
No doubt you could explain, tell me your story,
any story, say if I had failed you, or worse,
if you had gotten bored. Or maybe
it had less to do with me.

If only you offered language the world might
make sense, your parting words would shape
a planet in uninhabitable space.
Though I'd love the doomed terrain,
I'd say a clean goodbye to its seas and populations,
its beautiful long-necked birds.

But how can I speak of endings with one who's gone ahead?
Like wanting to call Bill and tell him that he died,
and how he died, and then he'd comfort me.
The suddenly dead don't take time out to reassure us.
I can't turn to you and say, help me,
you're my friend, make this unfriendliness easier.

But I want to. To fix things, cure abandonment.
The way a child keeps offering a parent all its love,
arms open, offering itself, though the parent
turned away years ago, for good.
Abandonment. Cruelty. Postcards from hell.
Keys to the door of endings.

Last night I was awakened by a loud, despairing voice,
a man's voice crying out, "Please forgive me!"
I feared for you, believed you, your utterly convincing call.
Should I try to save you? Slowly I realized this soul-cry
had come from me. I'm the only one here,
the only one living this body, this heart.

Moaning

Sure, pain tracks us down like a freight train—
but why rush out to greet it?
Why honeymoon at our demolition?

I can will it, this slo-mo ride
to being gutted. But why drive my ex-hope
down Volunteer and stop for you each time?

Freeze-frame me before I made my move
like a postcard of Niagara Falls frozen,
millions of pressurized tons stopped in ice.
See all those happy tourists tobogganing below!
Or at least freeze your *no* into one colossal jolt
instead of these cubes I keep melting
in my mouth.

Stop the past from hurtling forward.
Then you never said, "If you were younger. . . ."

Slammed against your sudden change of heart
I had to stop my car in the Plaza parking lot
try to remember why my body was
surrounding my heart.

I want to buy a ticket for the spring thaw.
The roar of Niagara will drown those happy sledders
if they don't get their asses out of town.
I want to moan like the Midnight Special—
a blues engine, one long wailing blotto:
one honey of a steel-throated sound
that won't slow down for you.

Why I Wear My Hair Long

I want to wrap it
around you
like a silk shirt

button it
slowly
carefully,

facing you
let the fringes
tickle your hips

until we ride
strong silken horses
glued on

& my flag
unfurls
a few strands

sticking
to your
lips.

Her Ex-husband

The last time I slept with
the ex-husband of a friend
I told myself, she's over him.
I was a bodybridge
over the moat of their separation.

This time I knew better.
But he ambushed me from behind
slid his hand down my hair,
down my back, low,
under pretext of helping me
better see Galway.
He was merely an usher,
helping my skin
see my desire for him.

Downhill like a skier
into the valley
he touched off a flash-dance
of premonition.
I could see the whole sordid history—
he was writing across me
to his ex-wife:

Hi Honey, I screwed your friend
and former teacher, the one
you placed on a pedestal—

I ran! Looked back at the waterslide
my body had become—
he had whipped up the lake,
the surrounding mountains

oxygen was in short supply
and there was no tram.

A New Way

It is hard.
Throbbing
          it is hard
to use throbbing
in a new way it is hard
to say throbbing
without using
teeth and lips and tongue
say throbbing
tongue between
teeth on
      throb
lips on *bing* it is hard
on the tongue to keep throbbing
when you are hard
a new
way say
when you are throbbing
and throbbing
and throbbing
and wet with new words
wet with new tongues
way way way in
a new
way to go
far in far out
come now
        you don't say

Mango Woman

How she
would
be
golden and sweet
a sugary sun
slipping under your
educated tongue,
how
she'd like the
licking of her
slick inner skin
the firm tip skimming
sheets of her sweetness
gentle teeth
teasing
tiny fibers of her
caught
for an instant
part of you
o taste &
swallow!
insistent
slippery and long
tongue-surfing over
luscious coral
over the hard core
I can't get enough
sounds urgent & strange
from your own
mouth
Ah!

Grrls: if you're home
alone
with a Duracel
tongue—
be the hungry one
eaten all up
all
gone.

Bad Sex

There's no such thing as bad whiskey or bad sex.
—Roland Flint, quoting a friend in L.A.

We were screamers that year.
Gina, the lady downstairs, told me
when we woke her and her truckdriving boyfriend,
she'd get angry with *him* about our shaking the house—
"Why can't you do that for *me?"*
1970, a year Reich would have envied.
Beethoven's Ninth in sex, loud, deaf to others,
Mike, the nineteen-year-old cowboy from Teaneck,
me, twenty-five.
Nights he didn't come five times he felt
pent up. For me,
it was the beginning of life in the body,
genesis, exodus from a dry marriage,
numbers and revelations.

Once, in a New Brunswick flophouse,
high noon, we sweated so hard the soaked sheets
slid off the plastic-covered
mattress and so did we. Wetness and the smell of sex
permeated the year like a rain forest.

How did it end? Tired.
In a frenzy of suspicion I read his diary—
I knew it! He'd cheated on me
with a woman from his office. She wore red gloves
he wrote, he came five times.

Now I'm older stats aren't the key.
Yet I hold to 1970, sex so good
my whole body and the next life and the next,
pre-reincarnated, came.
Even today I wear red gloves
as a tribute to that unknown woman
who took the next shift
and as a way of saying, thank you, Mike.

II. Double Vision

The White Zombie

Top left, our hero struggles to hold on
to his looks and his soul, but they are slipping
to the lower right of the screen, where he is pasty,
lackluster, with useless, sunken eyes.
The young Bella Lugosi (in his first movie!)
has stolen his soul. Once mindless,
he will push the heavy mill-wheel
with the club of the other zombies, creaking
round in bone-chilling sound, a source
of free labor forever.
"You'll be amazed how quickly you forget
the things you used to do,"
friends assured me.

At the top left, my face looks worried.
"I didn't want to lose contact with words
when I was pregnant," my poet friend told me.
Lower right, there's the radiant shell,
swathed in baby clothes and advice,
surrounded by the glowing pulp
of self-help magazines,
waiting to push the wheel.

The Dream

After nights of Lamaze and days
of layette sets,
I dream the dam breaks:
from back down the road
waters and rocks
rush toward me. I'm savvy,
having seen *Condominium*
and *Tidal Wave* on tv,
I run for high ground.
My belly and swollen feet slow
me down, though I escape into
Falwell's skyscraper, where
Jerry himself comforts me.
Distinguished, silvery-haired,
God holds my hand. When I wake up
the true disaster dawns on me:
I have been saved
despite being a Long Island Jew.
The dam I understand, but this?
As I fold the baby's clothes
I realize of course
I want to be born again,
to be fed, hugged, loved,
changed, and changed, and changed!

Letter On The Goddess

to Clayton Eshleman

The pregnancy has created in me a deep calm, which I love.
I have seen the Goddess twice, once in a treasure ship in our fields
behind the house, laden with furry white cows, magnolia trees
covered with snow on the leaves like little white gloves, black cats
with green eyes like the woods, and once waving in the icy arms
of trees as sunlight was striking them. These encounters leave me
strengthened, less fearful about giving birth since I have an ally.
The Goddess has royal blue eyebrows the color of her silk shorts,
and hyacinth nipples, though these change color with the weather
and her moods. She is never cold.

October Afternoon

I breathe in sleep
as the baby lies beside me,
her near-bald head nestled
in my arm, fragrant
with bits of down,
she drowses too, her nose
pressed to my breast.
The smell of milk spills
into her dreams, drugging
us both. The fumes of love
wrap thick around us,
and we are warm in the field
of our bodies.
There is no outside world,
no sudden leaves falling.
There is no sleep deeper
than this love.

Heather and the Wolf

All summer I've been too sick
to play with her, fighting with Lou.
He yells I should pull myself
together, stiff upper lip.

Too sick to play, fighting with Lou.
Heather won't sleep in her crib.
The wolf's outside, stiff upper lip.
In the dark it will get her.

Heather won't sleep in her crib.
All night the wolf's howling.
In the dark it will get her.
Heather howls, falls down stairs.

He yells I should pull myself
together, all summer I've been too sick.

Landscape With Bluebirds

Winter colorless after a long illness,
at last I see Paul Klee's "Landscape with Bluebirds,"
a score of red, green, and seablue trees,
a small blue mosque, canvas alive with color.

At last I see colors, Paul Klee's landscape alive
like the wrap of a woman washing clothes in the sun,
and a small blue mosque, a religion of color.
The text of his journal alongside: "Color possesses me."

Warm like the wrap of a Tunisian woman.
"I don't have to pursue it. . . . That is the meaning
of this happy hour." "Color possesses me."
"Color and I are one. I am a painter."

Red, green, seablue trees, bluebirds on clay roofs,
healing colors after a winter's long illness.

Lovers

Heather's hands are all over me like a lover's.
"Mama, Mama," she croons, loving the sounds.
Locked into each other's eyes, both of us laughing.
She smells so sweet, her skin's like vanilla.

"Mama, Mama," she croons. "Mmmm..."
After breakfast her pajamas smell like maple sugar.
She smells so sweet, her skin talcum and vanilla.
"Mama," she asks, "May I smell your nipple?"

Her pajamas smell like maple sugar.
I'm surprised, but "Sure, honey, how does it smell?"
"Mama, Mama, Mmmm..."
"It smells wonderful, Mama!"

Locked into each other's eyes, laughing together,
Heather's hands are all over me like a lover's.

Rhinoceroses

Knoxville Zoo

Sand-colored, at first you don't see them,
but then, "Oh my God!" something as big as my Honda
is nursing beside something the size
of a fuel truck. But they're alive!

My God! As big as my Honda.
Sand-sculpture wakes into moving shapes.
They're alive!
Do a slow-motion dance.

Sand-sculpture wakes into moving shapes.
Anne Bradstreet praised the Lord as a teat,
Do a slow-motion dance.
Here's proof she knew whereof she spoke.

Nursing at something the size of a fuel truck,
Sand-colored, at first you don't see them.

After Your Visit

For Robert Hass

Oh Bob, the voices that still live within us!
Rounding the curve at Blueridge,
it's 1968. I'm twenty.
My lover Jon Barefeet (yes!)
tells his mother, "You know what I hate most
about Marilyn? Her bourgeois morality!"
"I know," she responds.
I'm napping upstairs, but their voices carry
through an air vent.
Ten years later, his letter:
"I have a daughter now.
Her name is *Honey* in Sanskrit.
My anger against you has finally lifted."
Ten years more, I've lost his address.
Dear Jon, I'm ready to reply,
I too have a daughter. Being a mother
is a long process of healing. It's better now
than when we were together in one body.

Do present actions influence the past?
Can our words survive the sharp turns back?
Your poems return me to "small songs,"
"glistening wet wood."
Red Flame and Iceberg roses surround our house this May.
Heather skips across the grass, the grey cat in her arms.
"Mama, did you write a poem yet about the blue heron?"
Late afternoon, rounding the curve on Blueridge
I slow the car, Heather scans the reservoir
for our alphabet of birds.

Double Vision

Sweet Briar, Virginia

Heather, look! I catch myself
seeing with both your eyes and mine
though you're in Philadelphia—
                    There! Canadian geese,
with their black necks and white-striped chins.
The goslings stay close, fanning out from her.
See how the world's beauty has doubled for me
through you.
"Like seeing twice," Cézanne said of his love.

And there's this other double knowing
that you see things for yourself.
At nine, you still want time near me.
"Come with me to my room, Mama.
Mama, lie with me for awhile."
Soon you will push me away,
drawn toward the outskirts of the lake
navigating your own sleek life.

The world you have drawn for me
creates a bright circle, a new eye
making intimate connections.
It doesn't matter where we stand—
mother and babies a compass,
a clearing.

I have to be this far away
to give you this.

Prayer for *Chutzpah*

for Heather Miriam
with thanks to Jesse Graves

1.

Speaking the past to me between his verses,
Jesse could have stayed with "gorge"
for what the tunnel did to miners in
North Carolina, but he insisted on "mouth" too,
the lure of openings, then slow peristalsis,
the men of his family choking in its gut.

Where I grew up, working-class Oceanside,
gangs of black leather—The Lords, The Dukes,
did the swallowing up.
Girls were back-room trophies, we only had eyes,
we only had mouths for Sal, for Johnny.
A Jewish girl could not go far (thank God)—
not allowed to ride their hotrod Camaros.

Dark-eyed, long-lashed Camille Scaretta
was their virgin sacrifice, so beautiful
she got taken into the maw of gossip.
Camille, I should have spoken up for you.
The rest of us were bad-mouthed too.
The whole decade had been manhandled,
deserved its reputation,
what with bombs, walls, cyclone fences.
The world a bunch of thugs with guard-dogs.
We girls paid for power-lust on the local level.
We got screwed no matter what we didn't do.

Moving across the tracks, I was fodder
for my mother's mobility.
Rockville Center mouths were perfectly waxed,
ravenous for Saks Fifth Avenue.

Honey, if you didn't have money—
and we didn't—we were the Great Pretenders—
you had no mouth.
The *nouveau-riche* cliques sported matching knee-
socks and Garland sweaters. For them,
Hell was a long mall without Pappagallos.

2.

Camille, I'm calling you late, long-distance.
You will understand how Jeff Purchick
slow-danced me in his yellow crew-neck sweater—
warm welcome in that uptight town.
Wouldn't speak to me next day in homeroom.
Sue told me Jeff had done a background-check,
found out I'd made-out in my previous life
with a *wop*. I was untouchable then.
1962. We didn't know we were "the Sixties."
The Fifties held us by our Peter-Pan-
collared throats.

Another joke on us! Our family had moved
next door to a "restricted" country club.
Parker asked me for his ring back
two days before their prom.
Oh, he liked my Mango Sherbet lips.
He couldn't take a Jew.

3.

Walking alone at 5 a.m.
the clouds have misted the moon
but Jesse's word "mouth" makes me unsentimental
as ambition and rumor.
No black-lung disease, we were privileged.
We lived among color-coordinated sharks.

The boys in business suits
wielded better knives than switchblades.
Micky threatened me with a carving-knife
when I tried to leave his house.
Well-bred, he pressed the blade against his
own chest. Held me captive for hours.
Afterward he comissioned a gold charm,
a tape-recorder, as an apology.
The little reels spun until 1976.
Gold shot up and I sold it.

4.

Thank you, Jesse, for driving back
through that treacherous tunnel.
How much can be recovered in one man's quiet voice—
opening mine as loud as need be
to head through troubled memory and climb out.

And you, old moon, cratered sister,
thank you for an advance on destiny and choice.
Let my daughter speak from her self,
deal unsentimentally
with anyone who would swallow her.
Help her grow wild and smart,
hostage to no one, no one's charm.

Pre-dawn, September 13th,
a flock of cock-eyed geese are flying North,
their brash music the best accompaniment
to my unsentimental mouth,
to my prayer for *chutzpah*
for my daughter. If her gang goes
the wrong way, let her de-gorge it.
May her words be a tickertape parade
for her own flamboyant evolving.

December Journal

Gray and gray
    and the heart grows afraid
too many branches point downward
    phalanges of gray   switches
the witch's spell shoots
    forth more cold, banishing birds
nothing for the eye—

Now that the herd
    has been sold
oats along the roadside
    grow thick and high
pale silk brushes
    under last night's moon
sadness in such luxury
    uneaten
allowed to swell like an ocean

On the pasture road
    Anna in her red coat walks
deep in meditation   red earmuffs
    what music gathers her in?
Her white hair disappears
    past the tangles of brown boxwood.
The winter sun this morning
    not as bright as her hair
whiter than the memory
    of whiteness.

    Amazing!
A cardinal glows brighter
    amid brown branches,
Suddenly three red
    bellies round like fruit
but weightless, take flight

all flight
as if arriving when called for
an answer
on twigs too delicate
to hold anything but air

Hold still—
a flock of them!
Fifty maybe? walking
shining through brown
tangled branches
who no longer believes in
birdsign? Beauty
its own fortune
black beaks pecking the ground

Why not live outside the self?
hopping up branches like stairs
flying through tangled brush

Unscathed by briars
these will get through
to wake the world

Gone now
to the far trees
small as insects
did I imagine flight?

Red against gray
dazzling moments
swoop past—

Look! you tell yourself
as a mother might instruct a child
this is our world
isn't it ravishing?

Redbird

for Joelle and for Margo

Even the oaks shiver.
We suspect they dance in moonlight
the way our parents gave the best parties
while we slept—breathing, swaying.

Leaving our solitary rooms
two friends stride along the pasture road.
We inhabit this winter afternoon
in companionable silence—
not silence, but sky crossed with song,
mockingbirds answering over the trees.

A red gleam on the wire above
startles us—dazzled,
we laugh out loud.
Red gem against steel sky,
tiny heartbeat connecting me
to my friend, to my mother's
moonlit garden, to the winter afternoon.

...

The trees aren't stark,
we are, or what we've agreed
to call *the human heart*—
I've tried wrapping mine in silk,
freezing, spinning chic bandages.

Tried warming up with steaming
cups of love, little
marshmallows bobbing on top.
Opened my own shelter for

the loveless, no one should go
without.

Sing the old ballad,
Never enough.

...

Don't blame the briars
for the tattered cloak
of our mythologies.
We tear ourselves apart.
Trees haunted by our eyes.

Bare ruined choirs.
What he didn't give
comes back as damage.
Song of what has fallen
song of songs that fail to return.
Each bird a broken suitor.

Nothing there but trees.
So love them.
Romance a red herring.
It was never the prince
but the Mommy-grail we wanted.
What she couldn't give
comes back *stark.* As the world.

...

The mockingbird could have
been enough.

I could have learned a dozen other
songs through that one small body.
The snaky branches of the boxwood
spell the old alphabet
of mirrors looping to earth,
curving toward sky.
Sunlight on tulip bark
a moment's invitation to the dove.

The trees don't complain
about how little time
the birds spend in them.
They wait out the cold
don't judge the warmth scurrying
across their limbs.
Squirrels or crows,
skyward arch.

Crows and vultures pass over
like language without bitterness
medicine in flight.

...

Two women walk sounding out
their lives amid the more
rooted dancers
moving to an ordinary tune
companionable footsteps through the valley.
When do women stop dancing? one asks.
Redbird, when do we start?

III. Sentimental Talk

Unusual

1.

Cold white sun. Pam's off at the sperm bank
checking "Anglo-Saxon."
A wary shopper, she passed on the box marked
"unusual."
How sick I am of categories!
Do the trees care that the sky has no roots?
Pines and sky interplay, wincy winter blues.
Why not say "breath" for sky and branches?

Why call me "slow" when I may be racing toward
another life?
Oh, I can see myself in your rear-view mirror,
plucky like a sperm on my way to the bank,
determined, it's pay day,
breathe, breathe, wiggle wiggle, I'm an unusual
metaphor,
Reeboks instead of flagella.

Pam calls back—she's learned that "unusual"
means Native American.
It's 1933, Berlin, and I'm
unusual, hell, we're all a heartbeat away
from unusual. We all love our children past
categories, we'd invent any subterfuge to save them,
give them our breath, swallow this white sun,
dragons breathing fire on the Klan, a belch
for that boy
in Heather's class who said the Jews were stupid,
better save a candleflame for Mrs. English
so she'll recant the narrow outline
reteach the whole Fourth Grade—
this time that writing "off-topic"

is lovely, the practice of the outside lovely,
the practice of wind and trees and sun
unusual grandmothers and grandfathers
praying for the shining mothers and fathers
on our way to God-knows-where.

2.

In bed, when I tell him about my sperm-walk,
my concern about suddenly seizing the *macho*—
do I secretly want to be a man?
Lou says, "There's a big difference between
being a sperm and being a man."
"What's the difference?"
"A man is alive, a sperm, debatable."
"And sperm don't know where they're going,"
I add. "Neither do most men,"
says Lou.

The Genius Test, First Grade

Miss Howe let the lady take me
down to the basement
where we used to huddle for bomb drills.
"You were chosen for this test," she said.
"In your own words, tell me what this means:
An ill wind blows nobody good."

I was Miss Howe's pet, her
best reader, I loved her,
and I could feel
the sick wind filling me,
but I couldn't make my body speak
through my brain to this grim stranger.
My ordinariness hung over us,
blanketing our lungs and pores.
A failure at five. A dumb little fish.
She threw me back upstairs.

I didn't know it then
but in 1951 things were going badly
for artists in America
and things were about to get worse.
"President Eisenhower is eating bombs
for breakfast," *Life* would report.
Pediatrician Dr. William Carlos Williams
would never sit in his Poetry Office
at the Library of Congress, not
while paranoid fallout cloaked the House.

"Be quiet and put your heads down!"
Mr. Stone, our principal, walked
                              the stuccoed corridors,
a finger pressed to his lips.

When the town sirens blew
no one bothered to tell us
at Oceanside School Number Five
whether or not it was for real.

I planned on running home.
If I was going to die,
I wanted to be with my mother.
If it was the end of the world,
why keep still?

Not until years later did I hear:
It's an ill wind
                    that blows nobody good.
Senator McCarthy's black-and-white face
glaring in her livingroom
must have scared even the Testing Lady.
1951, we were huddled together,
there was no room for ambiguity
in a good American mouth.

Before the Discovery of the Mind

In his *Discovery of the Mind*
Bruno Snell traces the
birth of thought to Euripides,
arguing that there can be no
"mind" without a language
for reflection. Odysseus
was mindless, Athena on his shoulder
directing traffic for what
passed as ideas.

Wake up, Bruno!
Wasn't it that pooch Argus
who had the only memory
worth a damn? And don't thinking men
sometimes lack even an organic
concept of the body?

What do you yourself remember
about the woman who held you,
crooned to you, lifted you
from hunger to her breast?

And what of the night she
didn't come when you cried?
What sounds did the dark suck back in?
Did the little nightlight help you
with its domesticated face?

When they took that light
what stirred at the end of your bed?
To test your room you hurled the
picturebook near your pillow.
What did fright say
when the book hit something where
air should have been?

When she moved toward you
you could grasp—not her face,
but terror, her
shadowy body. Your own body
awakened like a mind.

When you tried to scream
it was one of those dreams
women have, sounds won't
form in the straining throat.

Many things have no language
for fear or reflection—the moon
in black, the witch who emerges
from the bedstead. In the movement from
the unknown to *God no*, there's a
lifetime of wiring the
moving dark to words.

If I could hold you, Bruno,
we could watch for
your terror, sing to her,
woo her,

Mama, don't hurt me,
Don't hate me or bite me.

In my own bad dream
she was already a tiger with
her mouth open wide
and the best I could do then
was be curious—
put my head in her mouth
(okay, it was dangerous,
but it was a way of going back in),
enter the circus performer's
fear of the trained beast.

Each time I stay longer
inside its breath,
less afraid of my own devouring.

Passover

My father heads our table,
his cheeks flushed from the first cup of wine.
At sunset he left his wallet upstairs
with bags of quarters from the vending machines.
He's making jokes and laughing with his mouth shut,
giving us his bright side—boy, clown, inventor.
Tonight by candlelight even the sullen teenagers
are cheerful, my sister Elaine and I,
glowing from apples and walnuts soaked in wine.
Aunt Marilyn is alive, sitting across from me.
Her breasts are hers again, untouched by cancer.
The New York Grandma is beside her
in a cotton housedress, two lines of berry lipstick
pressed on her faded mouth.
She's laughing, "Oy, stop it, Harry!" as my father
teases her. Letting go of want and pogroms.
My mother is no longer a martyr.
Pharoah has set her free so she can recline,
tasting her frothy matzoh-balls,
delighting in all she has created.
This is Passover, an invitation
to our freer selves to join us,
an invitation to the poor to come and dine.

My father loved kids, especially poor ones,
seeing himself starving back in Brooklyn.
He liked to buy ice cream for any hungry child
he found hanging around the stand.
The prayer book tells us, "The dead shall live on earth
in the good deeds they performed here,
and in the memory of those who live after them."
That's it, no big party, though this evening
circulating like sad music in the fragrant air
all the Jews who ever lived are still alive.

Once Upon A Time

In memory of my Father,
Harold Zimmerman

On your birthday I go to a gangster movie,
"Once Upon A Time in America," not knowing what I'm
in for. There are all these Italians playing Jews,
and De Niro's the spitting image of Uncle Nat. I watch
another movie inside of this one, listening to your
stories of childhood, machine guns gurgling in the East River,
your father's heart attack after he drowned your brother's
guns, Murder Incorporated, prohibition beer glasses
I still drink from believing you were more innocent
than your brothers. At ten, you must have been afraid
they would kill you, too. Why did your father drag you along
when he threw the guns off the bridge?

I look for you in the face of De Niro/Uncle Nat—
a scared kid in Brooklyn clinging to his mother haunted
by pogroms, mother scrubbing floors for a living, father off
in Hollywood selling his invention of animated cartoons,
father back in Brooklyn, broke, little sister hiding
from rapists in back of a second-hand store, brother
Sam stealing off trucks, and the oldest, Nat, a three-time
loser. All but one dead now, your sister of a lump
she was afraid to touch, Sam of cancer in his throat,
your mother dead of a broken heart to see her children go
before her, your father lost years before, his grief
flowing with the river over bullets.

You would have been sixty-four today, but the only one living
is Nat, in a trailor in California. Gray-haired,
probably a nice guy, the killing worn off with age,
with his son's overdose, his wife's amputated leg.
I look for you on the streets of New York but these
are Hollywood lots, I feel your frightened soul
behind the screen, and I miss you.
Tonight I dream I see the recently dead, but you are not
among them. It has been three years and the pain
is like a film, the voice behind the film is like the weather,
everywhere, but an absence.
I have to love myself, I look for what is left of you—
Uncle Nat, the stories.

Nothing Is So White

Nothing is so white
as the memory of whiteness

And blood is a ghost story
telling itself to the snow.
Weighted with this dust
the trees hang back,
hang fire, disintegrate—
collaborators with the snow
Antigone has been out again
covering her brother's skin
with one-to-two inches of
lightly packed powder.
My blood has gone gray.
Words sprinkle dust where
hands used to be. Where is the touch
that reached deep enough
to wake my body, and my dreams?

Easy Listening Music, 1-75

My father liked "easy listening
music"—everything else had been hard.
Work was his birthright.
His mother Anna scrubbed floors,
carrying her youngest, Harry.
His older brothers had opted out—
a small-time crook, a big shot
with Murder Incorporated. No wonder
my father was neat—no grime,
he was proud of his fingernails,
clean little moons over clean hands.

Why do I gather clutter?
Here she is, my Grandma Anna,
standing in the narrow aisle
of her second-hand store.
Anna, saver of old sweaters, mothballs,
pogroms hidden under mounds of cloth.
She hid her guitar on top of the hall closet.
We kids would have been embarrassed
to hear her sing Yiddish—
eager as my mother was to rise
to middle-class brightness.

What songs did my grandmother
take with her from Russia?
At fifteen, did she sing her mother's
lullabies in the ship's hold?
Croon them again to little Harry,

to Nat, and Sammy, and my frightened
                    Aunt Marilyn?
Were there other babies who didn't survive
hungry nights in Coney Island?

Markers for Indian mounds slip by,
this ground I ride easily over.

The Jewish graves are dispersed,
of Anna I have
no traces—only me.
I want to be a song my grandmother
would have recognized.

Rest a little, Harry.
Sleep, my little Anna,
Shayn viday-la vo-na,
pretty as the moon.

Sentimental Talk

My first husband is shorter now,
I lean on him looking down
as on an aging mother.
We are Mutt and Jeff in love,
stuck strolling
in self-satisfied sleep.
A kind of *hmm* comes off our bodies.

In waking life he's a urologist
remarried to an heiress.
I have to remind myself
that when we saw
A Doll's House
my husband exclaimed,
"They're just like us!"
That our marriage was a cave
on the fourteenth floor.
Now I seek a doctor in dreams,
one who will love me
and never leave me,
never bill me either.
The only way
to get decent medical care
is to marry it.
(I have to remind myself
it wouldn't fuck.)

The past is shorter now,
merely sentimental.
I have a family feeling
toward it in this
dream the way Verlaine
sang about Sundays with his wife:
In an old lonely
frozen park
two forms evoke the past.
Their eyes are dead
and their lips
are soft, and one
can hardly hear their words.

The Pocketbook

"Fluid Italian suede
in garnet,"
the copy croons.
I memorize
the Bergdorf Goodman
catalogue,
the blonde with garnet lips
carrying my pocketbook
against her slim hip.
370 dollars.
Half a rent check,
one chunk of my daughter's
college.
After weeks of foreplay
I sell out my family,
dial the toll-free number.
It's miraculously
easy, just "ten working-days"
and here it is, nestled
in a silk carrying-case
For days I hide it
behind the recliner,
playing *peek-aboo*,
trying it out when my husband's
not home.
Nothing else in my life's
this beautiful.
To keep it
I would have to buy
silk suits, tweed coats,
a silver Porsche,
house on Park Avenue.
My shoulders are unworthy
of the strap
in wine-red suede,
I would have to have inches

surgically added to my height.
"American women carry
their souls
in their pocketbooks,"
Edgar Allen Poe said.
Not just my soul,
my money,
my identity,
my credit cards.
This pocketbook soft and red
like a womb,
room where I would
carry myself in comfort,
be my own mother,
be drunk with color,
370 dollars.
I could sell my
wedding ring,
break into neighbors'
houses,
after two years
in the women's
correctional facility
there it would be
waiting for me,
fluid Italian suede
in garnet,
big enough to carry
the collected works of Poe,
o my fair sister, o my soul.

Heaven

Squaw Valley, California

1.

We expect our poets to feed us—
sushi, rare melon, but this was more
than we dreamed—Kinnell, sleeves
rolled up, apron tied, baseball cap, sweating
over coals—man! I knew I'd died
and gone to heaven when I bit into
Galway's burger—it gave *juicy*
new lips, teeth, tongue.
(Not to speak of the sausage.)

How could anyone not love him
with a redwood trunk
and the grill-savvy of Julia Child?
How could anyone not believe
in divine man when Galway flips
his burger for you?

2.

My father was from
Williamsburg, Brooklyn.
As a boy there were days
he didn't eat, not even potatoes
like those his mother dug,
a little girl in Minsk.

To say he worked his way out of
poverty doesn't touch
his lifelong fight for food
and steady ground.

We need new words for work,
as we need them for love.
(For my father these were the same.)

Barbeque a man's world
on middle-class Long Island,
where I grew up.

No matter how long
it took the coals, how
rare or burned the meat
Daddy was going to fix it.

Sometimes I think the hunger
will never stop.
I eat and eat
as if I were the immigrant
mother of my father,
the one who never had.

3.

Thank you dear poet,
for the cracked
crust
where the muse can feed on
me—

Thank you for
my father in your
sweet face and strong
working hands.

The words will last.
Delicious!

Why Not Blossom Instead?

The natural world
is a spiritual house—

intimate as skin, made of
dawn, evening light, purple stars,
invisible poets whose voices reach me
through tiny petalled mikes.
I'm speaking with William Stafford again.

He says what I need to hear:
"It's okay that you didn't win.
Why hang your ego on that hook?
Why not blossom lightly
from a pink dogwood?" Dutifully
I protest that I'm Jewish,
the dogwood is linked to the story of Christ.

"Trees are non-denominational,"
he laughs. He's as real to me as this
bed of wildflowers, this late sun
a goblet of apricot liqueur.

A river of violets answers when I look for
more of him.
I turn to the flowers for advice
an old friend might have offered.
An unusual animal chirps from the grass:
"So, your husband wanted this
victory for you? Whisper the truth
over him. Make corsages
of it, make forests filled with mutual sprays
of untamed blooms.
Call the wildest orchid *Losing*."

Out of Bondage

He was into
bondage and I
couldn't tie
the knots,
isn't that
the shortest
short story
you ever heard?

Tighter even than
*"Speak, if you're
a Kiowa."*

Silence.

*The arrow went
straight to
the enemy's
heart.*

(and
his name,
I swear to God
was Slideman!)

Ah, the power of
language,
the pointed
tongue-to-the-heart
& the more slippery tongue—

trust me, you don't *know*
from slippery
unless you're that
frustrated fish floundering
out of a slip-knot
on and off
a waterbed.

Dear Orpheus

Don't look
back this time,
ok, babe?
It gets wearing—
the shrieking
the tearing of limbs
stupid Furies
imitating
earthbound hacks.
Not to mention
the commute—
hell
& back
more predictable
than Amtrak.

Don't think
I'm not grateful
for these
forays—
it's just
I'm getting older
(what hell *is*, darling)
nothing new
to wear—
basic black's dowdy,
overdone.

At least let me
go first.
I'll know
better than to
glance back
when you call—

but oh! those dangling
apples big as tires
in your vowels.
Boys in sunglasses
and warm leather
the syllables
of my name
sips of ouzo
from your mouth. . . .

So what if I blow it
I've been
torn to pieces
by love before
my arms know how to swim
my head knows how to sing
and I
don't mind
waking up
in fragments.

It's your turn
to silently biodegrade
into a sea
of boring
mist.

I'll
myth you.

IV. How to Get Heat Without Fire

Fireflies

In the dry summer field at nightfall,
fireflies rise like sparks.
Imagine the presence of ghosts
flickering, the ghosts of young friends,
your father nearest in the distance.
This time they carry no sorrow,
no remorse, their presence is so light.
Childhood comes to you.
memories of your street in lamplight,
holding those last moments before bed,
capturing lightning-bugs,
with a blossom of the hand
letting them go. Lightness returns,
an airy motion over the ground
you remember from *ring-around-the-rosie*.
If you stay, the fireflies become fireflies
again, not part of your stories,
as unaware of you as sleep, being
beautiful and quiet all around you.

The Ladies

August, Montgomery, Alabama

98° and the dogs
are digging holes
to cool their
bottoms in
  mining
    digging
you write of
your search for
    your father's past
in the coal mines
of Harlan
& what we do
to each other
in the 100° heat
digging,
wanting to go
    deeper,
even with the
shades closed
to hide your
married body
my unmarried skin
digging each other
the neighbors
so mean so
    stupid
they don't take
their dogs in
the ladies wonder
what the beasts are doing
beat them for holes
in the yard
for their urge to find shade
& dig

Black Bean Soup

Black bean soup, and my mother's nineteen again.
A *whirr* of fans—it's summer in Havana.
Three women share a huge, tiled room overlooking
the Prado. "That was fifty years ago."

In Battista's Cuba, the best time of her life.
"Men handed us chocolates and flowers
as we strolled the Prado.
The chocolates had liqueurs in them."

"They loved Americans then."
Young men from New Orleans whirled them
to nightclubs. Even the chocolates were loaded.
"I didn't want to go home. Nothing for me

in Montgomery." In Havana she rhumbaed all night.
"Next summer I sailed the *Marguerita* to Colombia.
The President of Panama's son took me dancing.
'Rodriguez Parras,'" she rolls the *r*'s on her tongue.

"We met on the boat to Baranquilla.
Our guide asked, 'Do the ladies want to see
a whorehouse?' The girls wore kimonos in the afternoon,
red carnations in their window-boxes."

"They gathered around to say hello.
I don't know, maybe they were paid to be polite.
Potted red carnations in their back windows.
It was just another profession."

"Like being a secretary, treated well in town.
Once we walked through Cienaga in our bathing suits,

the '*policia*' in back of us.
Why we were arrested? 'No hablo espanol!'"

"They threw us in jail.
I was wearing a white terrycloth cape.
Indecent exposure! The chief spoke English.
He let us go just in time for our boat."

"Rodriguez Parras."
She rolls the *r*'s luxuriously over her tongue.
Three women look out on the Prado.
Black bean soup, and my mother's nineteen again.

Entering the Blue Room at Ragdale

The falling light reminds me of an old house
on Lake Seneca, where light was a friend,
dependable, gray most days, gold some.
Through the half-open door to the porch
the hammock is empty and thin.
Once it was plumped with us, almost lovers.

Now there is only light in the swing.
Prairie murmurs spread against the garden.
Around the house shade trees grow darker,
hundreds of years old in late summer.

Hunger

Clouds so flat
unmoving
they make me feel faint
my southern mother never
made potato pancakes
but my Brooklyn-born
father did

Once or twice on a
Long Island Sunday
there was a certain music
in all the grating,
even in the sour cream
(now he doesn't make them)

My father's mother
from Russia-Brooklyn
made terrific latkes
(he said) they were a dream
she taught him

"They have to have blood
from the knuckles grated
into them
to make them authentic"

From an old Yiddish saying
I feared the food a little

Yahrzeit, For My Father

Harold Zimmerman
1919-1980

I burned your candle in a tin can
from Israel, it was the only one
the temple had left.
"Burns 26 hours," the wrapper says,
"Magnified and Sanctified
by the name of God."
"Tomb of Rabbi Meir Bal-Hanes,"
(with a picture, palm tree, orange sky.)
Two years ago today
Gutterman's handed my sister your ashes
in what looked like a coffee can.
Later we buried a dead sparrow in the yard.
You used to feed the birds.
We needed to give ourselves
the comfort of dirt.

What happened to thick glass,
giving memory sight?
Grandmother candles, grandfather candles
at home on the mantle,
flames that burned all day with shadows.

What happened to you?

At the funeral home they were ready
to box you without shoes.
"It doesn't matter, his feet won t show."
I remember your telling us
about your father's
Brooklyn grave,
how the rabbi charged more
than you could pay
to pray for him.
We went home and got your good shoes.

The Only Way

In memory of May Sarton, 1912-1995

Pale wheat before the black mountain
a quick flock of wrens—
I meet you again in a house of gathering.

The lights are on, May,
the pines greener in winter light.
I come to you alone, the only way.

The busy world falls away
in the presence of mountains.
The world stripped down for light.

How long it has taken me
to say goodbye! You were not easy.
Your words scalded me.

When love's gone I need you most.
You always met me there—
raged at anyone who hurt me.

In my grief, you were mine.
Now you are loss too.
The light goes, the branches darken.

Stay with me awhile
in the low sky and mountains.
Wrens rest in the boxwood.

Then they are simply not there.
Absence and presence
fixed lightly to their wings.

Bill

In Memory of William Stafford, 1914-1993

As the green hills unfold
beneath the Cumberland's gray skies
I know you're in there, Bill,
in the clouds and pale rolls of hay
ready to be carted off to barns,

in the rhythmical earth underneath
the roadways. You're the quiet
within this quiet evening.
Am I confusing you with God?

You'd rather be the weathered wood
in a cantilevered barn,
gray slats mirroring strips of clouds.

You're here in the evening air,
the field, the sky,
the surrounding mountains,
the water jar, the shade.

In The Face Of Solitude

I keep my body here, with me,
reaching out to the still air,
trying to smash the stillness out,
tearing the air's silk
to find out what's beating there.

Stripped to the voice,
who will I be
in the face of solitude?
I am frightened by my skin
that cannot escape.

What is denied to love:
"a fin in a waste of waters,"
the pen in its wake.
The sky goes so slowly,
& the body goes fast.

How To Get Heat Without Fire

Beneath the dark floor
there has always been love,
but the trick is
how to get down to it?
Shall I tear my way down
like a tiger clawing
the floorboards, when this
tearing down is what scarred you?
Whose mother is there
in the dark trying hard
to hide you from the memory
of the floorboards in flame?
How to get heat without fire?
To coax light open?
To ease you new into
the world if I am not
a mother, or a beloved?
Pull back? Peel back dead
bark, pull back the boards
we trample, throw each other
down on and through some days?
Turn the floor into a pool
we can dive deep into,
cradle the mothers,
let the animals swim their ways?
Has music ever saved anyone?
Then I will reenter my life
as sound,
as notes strung like pearls
that you have yearned
to enter.
I will be sound,
I will be sound,
and silence,
listening.

About the Author

Marilyn Kallet was born in Montgomery, Alabama, and grew up in New York. She attended Jackson College/Tufts University, and received her M.A. and Ph.d. in Comparative Literature from Rutgers.

Kallet is Professor of English and Director of the Creative Writing Program at the University of Tennessee in Knoxville. She is the author of seven books, including three volumes of poetry, translations, criticism, and anthologies. Most recently, she co-edited with Patricia Clark *Worlds in Our Words: Contemporary American Women Writers*, Blair Press/Prentice Hall, 1996. She also edited *A House of Gathering: Poets on May Sarton's Poetry*, UT Press, 1993. Her poems have been published in *New Letters, Hawaii Review, Denver Quarterly, International Quarterly*, and many other literary magazines. In 1988 she won the Tennessee Arts Commission Literary Fellowship in poetry. With Judith Ortiz Cofer, Kallet is currently editing a volume of personal essays: *Sleeping With One Eye Open: A Survival Guide for Creative Women*.